Enduring Words

FOR THE

LEADER

Enduring Words
FOR THE
LEADER

School Specialty.
Publishing

School Specialty
Publishing

Anthology: Margaret Miller
Design: Zoë Murphy

This anthology © The Five Mile Press Pty Ltd

This edition published in the United States in 2006 by School Specialty
Publishing, a member of the School Specialty Family.

Library of Congress Cataloging-in-Publication Data is on file with the publisher.

Send all inquiries to:

School Specialty Publishing
8720 Orion Place
Colombus, OH 43240-2111

ISBN 0-7696-4745-6

Printed in China
1 2 3 4 5 6 7 8 9 FMP 09 08 07 06 05

www.SchoolSpecialtyPublishing.com

CONTENTS

Preface

What Makes a Leader?

Leaders on Leadership

A Matter of Character

Getting the Best From Others

Opportunity and Risk

How to Get to the Top

Wise Words From Leaders

PREFACE

The desire to have someone to look up to and admire is a part of the human condition. *Enduring Words for the Leader* celebrates the leaders who elicit this admiration in others—those who lead in education, business, athletics, and religious institutions and those who lead and inspire simply by living exemplary lives.

There is no simple definition that encompasses all that it means to be a good leader. And all good leaders do not embody the same characteristics. For this reason, the quotations in this beautiful anthology reflect a variety of perspectives on leadership that all prove true universally.

A vital part of being a good leader is the ability to work effectively with others in order to achieve lofty goals. A great leader brings out the best in others, inspiring in them talents they may not have known they possessed. This anthology pays tribute to these leaders.

In the end, a good leader may possess wonderful charisma, unparalleled talent, and unremitting energy; yet, the good leader's true worth lies in his or her integrity, humanity, and moral strength. Above all else, these are the principles most honored in *Enduring Words for the Leader*.

What Makes a Leader?

Leadership is practiced

not so much in words

as in attitude and in actions.

Harold S. Geneen, 1910–1997
American businessman

The final test of a leader

is that he leaves behind him in other men

the conviction and the will to carry on.

The genius of a good leader

is to leave behind him a situation

which common sense, with the grace of genius,

can deal with successfully.

Walter Lippman, 1889–1974
American journalist, political commentator

We herd sheep,

we drive cattle,

but we lead people.

Lead me, follow me,

or get out of my way.

General George S. Patton, 1885–1945
American military leader

$\mathcal{T}$he real leader

has no need to lead –

he is content to point the way.

Henry Miller, 1891–1980
American writer

When you come into the presence of a leader of men,

you know that you have come into the presence of fire –

that it is best not incautiously to touch that man,

that there is something that makes it

dangerous to cross him.

Woodrow Wilson, 1856–1924
President of the United States of America

I cannot trust a man

to control others

who cannot control himself.

General Robert E. Lee, 1807–1870
American military leader

$\mathcal{A}$ leader must have

the courage to act

against an expert's advice.

James Callaghan, 1912–2005
British Prime Minister

The leader can never close the gap
between himself and the group.
If he does, he is no longer what he must be.
He must walk a tightrope between
the consent he must win
and the control he must exert.

Vince Lombardi, 1913–1970
American football coach

Leaders create

an environment in which everyone

has the opportunity to do work

which matches their potential capabilities

and for which an equitable differential reward

is provided.

Elliott Jaques, 1917–2003
American psychologist

*A*uthority poisons
everybody who takes authority
upon himself.

Golda Meir, 1898–1978
Israeli Prime Minister

The chief executive who knows
his strengths and weaknesses as a leader
is likely to be far more effective
than the one who remains blind to them.
He also is on the road to humility –
that priceless attitude of openness to life
that can help a manager absorb mistakes,
failures, or personal shortcomings.

John Adair, 1913–1997
American anthropologist

The commander must decide
how he will fight the battle
before it begins .... He must make the enemy
dance to his tune from the beginning
and not vice versa.

Viscount Montgomery, 1887–1976
English field marshal

The measure of great leaders is their success in bringing everyone around to their opinion twenty years later.

Ralph Waldo Emerson, 1803–1882
American essayist, philosopher

*A*sking who ought to be the boss

is like asking who ought to be

the tenor in the quartet.

Obviously, the man

who can sing tenor.

———————————
Henry Ford, 1863–1947
American automobile manufacturer

*T*he secret of a leader

lies in the tests he has faced

over the whole course of his life

and the habit of action

he develops

in meeting those tests.

Gaily Sheehy, b. 1937
American author, social critic

*P*eople ask the difference
between a leader and a boss.
The leader works in the open,
and the boss is covert.
The leader leads,
and the boss drives.

Theodore Roosevelt, 1858–1919
President of the United States of America

A leader has the vision and conviction

that a dream can be achieved.

He inspires the power and energy

to get it done.

Ralph Lauren, b. 1939
American clothes designer

Who hath not served

cannot command.

John Florio, 1553–1625
English writer

$\mathcal{L}$eaders are problem solvers

by talent and temperament

and by choice.

Harlan Cleveland, b. 1938
American-born political scientist

The first thing
a great person does
is make us realize
the insignificance
of circumstance.

Ralph Waldo Emerson, 1803–1882
American essayist, philosopher

The most effective leader is the one who satisfies the psychological needs of his followers.

David Ogilvy, 1911–1999
American advertising company owner, lecturer

$\mathcal{N}$o man will make a great leader

who wants to do it all himself

or to get all the credit

for doing it.

Andrew Carnegie, 1835–1919
Scottish-born American businessman, philanthropist

*H*e that would govern others

first should be master of himself.

Philip Massinger, 1583–1640
English dramatist, poet

The best method for estimating the intelligence of a ruler is to look at the men he has around him.

Niccolo Machiavelli, 1469–1527
Italian diplomat, political philosopher, writer

Leadership

is the art of getting someone else

to do something you want done

because he wants to do it.

Dwight D. Eisenhower, 1890–1969
President of the United States of America

*L*eadership is getting someone

to do what they don't want to do,

to achieve what they want to achieve.

Tom Landry, 1924–2000
American football player

*L*eaders are the custodians of a nation's ideals,

of the beliefs it cherishes, of its permanent hopes,

of the faith which makes a nation

out of a mere aggregation of individuals.

Walter Lippman, 1889–1974
American journalist, political commentator

*O*ur chief want

is someone

who will inspire us

to be what we know

we could be.

Ralph Waldo Emerson, 1803–1882
American essayist, philosopher

A leader is one who,

out of madness or goodness,

volunteers to take upon himself

the woe of the people.

There are few men so foolish,

hence the erratic quality of

leadership in the world.

John Updike, b. 1932
American writer, poet, critic

The greatness of a leader

is measured by the achievements of the led.

This is the ultimate test of his effectiveness.

General Omar Bradley, 1893–1981
American field commander

*T*he ability to deal with people

is as purchasable a commodity

as sugar or coffee,

and I will pay more for that ability

than for any other under the sun.

John D. Rockefeller, 1874–1960
American oil millionaire, philanthropist

Leadership is not magnetic personality —
that can just as well be a glib tongue.
It is not making friends and influencing people —
that is flattery.
Leadership is lifting a person's vision to higher sights,
the raising of a person's performance
to a higher standard,
the building of a personality
beyond its normal limitations.

Peter Drucker, 1909-2005
American management theorist

$\mathcal{P}$ower is strength and the ability

to see yourself through your own eyes

and not through the eyes of another.

It is being able to place

a circle of power at your own feet

and not take power

from someone else's circle.

Marian Anderson, 1902–1993
American singer

$\mathcal{M}$en shrink less

from offending one who inspires love

than one who inspires fear.

Niccolo Machiavelli, 1469–1527
Italian diplomat, political philosopher, writer

A boss creates fear,

a leader confidence.

A boss fixes blame;

a leader corrects mistakes.

A boss knows all;

a leader asks questions.

A boss makes work drudgery;

a leader makes it interesting.

A boss is interested in himself or herself;

a leader is interested in a group.

Unknown

I have three precious things

which I hold fast and prize.

The first is gentleness;

the second is frugality;

the third is humility ....

Be gentle and you can be bold;

be frugal and you can be liberal;

avoid putting yourself before others

and you can become

a leader among men.

Lao-Tzu, c. 4 BC
Chinese philosopher

The very essence of leadership

is that you have to have vision.

You can't blow an uncertain trumpet.

Theodore M. Hesburgh, 1917–1999
American clergyman

*T*he king

is the man who can.

Thomas Carlyle, 1795–1881
Scottish philosopher, author

$\mathcal{L}$eadership is the ability

to put the right people

in the right jobs

and then sit on the sidelines

and be a rousing good

cheerleader.

Anonymous

The task of the leader

is to get his people from where they are

to where they have not been.

Henry Kissinger, b. 1923
American Secretary of State

A leader is a man

who assumes responsibility.

He says, 'I was beaten.'

He does not say,

'My men were beaten.'

Antoine de Saint Exupery, 1900–1944
French aviator, writer

To lead people, walk beside them ….

As for the best leaders,

people do not notice their existence.

The next best, people honor and praise.

The next, people fear.

And the next, people hate.

When the best leader's work is done,

people think they've done it themselves.

Lao-Tzu, c. 4 BC
Chinese philosopher

*Y*ou don't manage people;

you manage things.

You lead people.

Admiral Grace Hooper, 1906–1992
American navy officer

Leadership can be thought of as a capacity to define oneself to others in a way that clarifies and expands a vision of the future.

Edwin H. Friedman, 1932–1996
American family therapist, rabbi

*Every age needs men
who will redeem the time
by living with a vision
of things that are to be.*

Adlai Stevenson, 1900–1965
American lawyer, statesman, United Nations ambassador

$\mathcal{T}$he quality of leaders

is reflected in

the standards they set

for themselves.

Ray Kroc, 1902–1984
American founder of McDonald's

I start with the premise

that the function of leadership

is to produce more leaders,

not more followers.

Ralph Nader, b. 1934
American activist, lawyer

*T*he best job

goes to the person who can get it done

without passing the buck

or coming back with excuses.

Abraham Lincoln, 1809–1865
President of the United States of America

*L*eaders must invoke

an alchemy

of great vision.

Henry Kissinger, b. 1923
American Secretary of State

*Reason and judgment
are the qualities
of a leader.*

Tacitus, 56–117 AD
Roman historian

*S*ingleness of purpose

is one of the

chief essentials

for success in life

no matter what

one's aim may be.

John D. Rockefeller, 1874–1960
American oil millionaire, philanthropist

*L*eaders are made;

they are not born.

They are made by hard effort,

which is the price which

all of us must pay

to achieve any goal

that is worthwhile.

Vincent Lombardi, 1913–1970
American football coach

*N*o general in the midst of battle

has a great discussion about

what he is going to do if he is defeated.

David Owen, b.1938
British politician

$\mathcal{T}$ime is neutral

and does not change things.

With courage and initiative,

leaders change things.

Jesse Jackson, b. 1941
American civil rights leader, political activist

$\mathcal{T}$he art of leadership

is saying no, not yes.

It is very easy to say yes.

Tony Blair, b. 1953
British Prime Minister

A prime function of a leader
is to keep hope alive.

_____

John W. Gardner, 1912–2002
American Secretary of Health, Education, and Welfare

It is better to have

a lion at the head of an army of sheep

than a sheep at the head of an army of lions.

_____

Arab saying

$\mathcal{T}$o strive,

to seek,

to find,

and not to yield.

Lord Alfred Tennyson, 1809–1892
English poet

A leader takes people

where they want to go.

A great leader takes people

where they don't necessarily want to go

but ought to be.

Rosalynn Carter, b.1927
First Lady of the United States of America

Leaders on Leadership

A true leader always keeps

an element of surprise up his sleeve,

which others cannot grasp,

but which keeps his public

excited and breathless.

Charles de Gaulle, 1890–1970
French statesman, general

$\mathcal{B}$efore you can inspire with emotion,

you must be swamped with it yourself.

Before you can move their tears,

your own must flow.

To convince them,

you must yourself believe.

Sir Winston Churchill, 1874–1965
British Prime Minister, statesman, writer

Nothing is more difficult,

and therefore more precious,

than to be able to make decisions.

Napoleon Bonaparte, 1769–1821
French emperor

If you lead a country like Britain,

a strong country, a country which has taken a lead

in world affairs in good times and in bad,

a country that is always reliable,

then you have to have a touch of iron.

Baroness Margaret Thatcher, b. 1925
British Prime Minister

I suppose leadership

at one time meant muscles;

but today it means

getting along with people.

Indira Gandhi, 1917–1984
Prime Minister of India

I know I have the body of
a weak and feeble woman, but I have
the heart and stomach of a King,
and of a King of England, too.

Elizabeth I, 1533–1603
Queen of England

I believe in

benevolent dictatorship

provided I am the dictator.

Richard Bronson, b. 1950
British entrepreneur

A leader or a man of action in a crisis almost always acts subconsciously and then thinks of the reasons for his actions.

Jawaharlal Nehru, 1889–1964
Indian statesman

As we are liberated

from our own fear,

our presence automatically

liberates others.

Nelson Mandela, b. 1918
President of South Africa

$\mathcal{T}$here are two levers

for moving men –

interest and fear.

Napoleon Bonaparte, 1769–1821
French emperor

*G*reat spirits have always found violent opposition from mediocrities. The latter cannot understand it when a man does not thoughtlessly submit to hereditary prejudices but honestly and courageously uses his intelligence.

Albert Einstein, 1879–1955
German-born American physicist

A good head

and a good heart

are a formidable combination.

Nelson Mandela, b. 1918
President of South Africa

To change your mind
and defer to correction
is not to sacrifice your independence;
for such an act is your own,
in pursuance of your own impulse,
your own judgment,
and your own thinking.

Marcus Aurelius, 121–180 AD
Roman emperor, philosopher

We're all worms,

but I do believe

I'm a glow-worm.

Sir Winston Churchill, 1874–1965
British Prime Minister, statesman, writer

$\mathcal{A}$ leader, once convinced

that a particular course of action

is the right one,

must be undaunted

when the going gets tough.

Ronald Reagan, 1911–2004
President of the United States of America

*L*eadership and learning

are indispensable to each other.

John F. Kennedy, 1917–1963
President of the United States of America

A leader

is a dealer

in hope.

Napoleon Bonaparte, 1769–1821
French emperor

If your actions inspire others to

dream more, learn more,

do more, and become more,

you are a leader.

John Quincy Adams, 1767–1848
President of the United States of America

$\mathscr{S}$urround yourself

with the best people you can find,

delegate authority,

and don't interfere.

———————————

Ronald Reagan, 1911–2004
President of the United States of America

$\mathcal{S}$how me someone without an ego,

and I'll show you a loser.

I'll stay until I'm tired of it.

So long as Britain needs me,

I shall never be tired of it.

Baroness Margaret Thatcher, b. 1925
British Prime Minister

I am a leader by default,

only because nature

does not allow a vacuum.

Desmond Tutu, b. 1931
South African bishop

*T*he day soldiers stop bringing you their problems

is the day you have stopped leading them.

They have either lost confidence

that you can help them

or concluded that you do not care.

Either case is a failure of leadership.

Colin Powell, b. 1937
United States Secretary of State

A leader who doesn't hesitate

before he sends

his nation into battle

is not fit to be a leader.

Golda Meir, 1898–1978
Russian-born Israeli stateswoman

$\mathcal{N}$ever give an order

that can't be obeyed.

General Douglas MacArthur, 1880–1964
American military leader

$\mathcal{Y}$ou do not lead

by hitting people over the head –

that's assault, not leadership.

Dwight D. Eisenhower, 1890–1969
President of the United States of America

I have never accepted

what many people kindly said,

namely that I have inspired the nation.

It was the nation

and the race dwelling all around the globe

that had the lion heart.

I had the luck to be called upon

to give the roar.

Sir Winston Churchill, 1874–1965
British Prime Minister, statesman, writer

A Matter of Character

$\mathcal{L}$eadership is a combination

of strategy and character.

If you must be without one,

be without the strategy.

General H. Norman Schwarzkopf, b. 1934
American military leader

I hope I shall possess firmness and virtue

enough to maintain what I consider

the most enviable of all titles,

the character of an honest man.

George Washington, 1732–1799
President of the United States of America

In matters of style,

swim with the current;

in matters of principle,

stand like a rock.

Thomas Jefferson, 1743–1826
President of the United States of America

I desire to so conduct

the affairs of this administration

that if at the end,

when I come to lay down the reins of power,

I have lost every other friend on earth,

I shall at least have one friend left,

and that friend shall be deep down

inside of me.

Abraham Lincoln, 1809–1865
President of the United States of America

*E*thics must begin

at the top of an organization.

It is a leadership issue,

and the chief executive

must set the example.

Edward Hennessy, b. 1942
American lawyer

*O*bserve good faith

and justice towards all nations.

Cultivate peace and

harmony within.

George Washington, 1732–1799
President of the United States of America

*G*od grant

that men of principle

shall be our principal men.

Thomas Jefferson, 1743–1886
President of the United States of America

$\mathcal{P}$ress on steadily,

keep to the straight road

in your thinking and doing,

and your days will ever flow on smoothly.

The soul of man … can never

be thwarted from without,

and its good consists in righteousness

of character and action

and in confining every wish thereto.

Marcus Aurelius, 121–180 AD
Roman emperor, philosopher

*The ultimate measure of a man
is not where he stands in moments
of comfort and convenience,
but where he stands at times
of challenge and controversy.*

Martin Luther King, Jr., 1929–1968
American civil rights leader, minister

The supreme quality for a leader is unquestionable integrity. Without it, no real success is possible, no matter whether it is in a section gang, on a football field, in an army, or in an office. If his associates find him guilty of phoniness, if they find that he lacks forthright integrity, he will fail. His teachings and actions must square with each other. The first great need, therefore, is integrity and high purpose.

Dwight D. Eisenhower, 1890–1969
President of the United States of America

$\mathcal{L}$et us raise a standard

to which the wise and honest can repair;

the rest is in the hands of God.

George Washington, 1732–1799
President of the United States of America

If you have no character to lose,
people will have no faith in you.

Mahatma Gandhi, 1869–1948
Indian statesman, philosopher

$\mathcal{I}$do the very best I know how –

the very best I can;

and I mean to keep on doing it

until the end.

Abraham Lincoln, 1809–1865
President of the United States of America

Each time a man stands up for an ideal

or acts to improve the lot of others

or strikes out against an injustice,

he sends forth a tiny ripple of hope ....

Those ripples build a current

that can sweep down the mightiest walls

of oppression and resistance.

Robert F. Kennedy, 1925–1967
American senator

Try not to become a man of success

but rather a man of value.

Albert Einstein, 1879–1955
German-born American physicist

*A*chievement of your happiness
is the only moral purpose of your life,
and that happiness,
not pain or mindless self-indulgence,
is the proof of your moral integrity
since it is the proof and the result of your
loyalty to the achievement of your values.

Ayn Rand, 1905–1982
American writer

$\mathscr{Y}$ou gain strength, courage, and confidence

by every experience in which you really stop

to look fear in the face.

You must do the thing you cannot do.

Eleanor Roosevelt, 1884–1962
First Lady of the United States of America, writer, diplomat

*H*appiness and moral duty
are inseparably connected.

George Washington, 1732–1799
President of the United States of America

*C*haracter is like a tree and

reputation like its shadow.

The shadow is what we think of it;

the tree is the real thing.

Abraham Lincoln, 1809–1865
President of the United States of America

*N*ever value the advantages derived
from anything involving breach of faith,
loss of self-respect, hatred, suspicion,
or execration of others,
insincerity, or the desire for something
to be veiled and curtained.

Marcus Aurelius, 121–180 AD
Roman emperor, philosopher

$\mathscr{I}$ can honestly say that I was never affected

by the success of an undertaking

if I felt it was the right thing to do,

if I was for it,

regardless of the possible outcome.

Golda Meir, 1898–1978
Israeli Prime Minister

$\mathcal{I}$ love the name of honor

more than I fear death.

Julius Caesar, 100–44 BC
Roman emperor

*O*ur days begin to end

the day we become silent

about things that matter.

Martin Luther King, Jr., 1929–1968
American civil rights leader, minister

Getting the Best From Others

*T*reat people as if
they were what they ought to be,
and you help them to become what
they are capable of being.

Johann Wolfgang von Goethe, 1749–1832
German poet, writer, dramatist, scientist

*T*he best executive is the one

who has the sense enough to pick good men

to do what he wants done

and the self-restraint

to keep from meddling with them

while they do it.

Theodore Roosevelt, 1858–1919
President of the United States of America

$\mathcal{T}$he chief lesson I have learned in a long life

is that the only way to make a man trustworthy

is to trust him;

and the surest way to make him untrustworthy

is to distrust him and show your mistrust.

Henry L. Stimson, 1867–1950
American statesman

$\mathscr{I}$f you tell people

where to go,

but not how to get there,

you'll be amazed

at the results.

General George S. Patton, 1885–1945
American military leader

$\mathscr{S}$ix traits of effective leaders:

Make others feel important.

Promote a vision.

Follow the golden rule.

Admit mistakes.

Criticize others only in private.

Stay close to the action.

Christian Nevell Bovee, 1820–1904
American lawyer, author

The high sentiments always win in the end;

the leaders who offer blood, toil, tears, and sweat

always get more out of their followers

than those who offer safety and a good time.

When it comes to the pinch,

human beings are heroic.

George Orwell, 1903–1950
English writer, critic

A reflective reading of history will show

that no man ever rose to military greatness

who could not convince his troops

that he put them first

above all else.

General Maxwell Taylor, 1901–1987
American military leader, diplomat

Always do everything

you ask of those

you command.

General George S. Patton, 1885–1945
American military leader

$\mathcal{T}$he secret of successful managing

is to keep the five guys

who hate you

from the four guys who

haven't made up their minds.

Casey Stengel, 1890–1975
Manager of the New York Mets

If you want to build a ship,
don't herd people together to collect wood,
and don't assign them tasks and work,
but rather teach them to long for
the endless immensity of the sea.

Antoine de Saint Exupery, 1900–1944
French aviator, writer

$\mathcal{Y}$ou cannot push anyone up the ladder

unless he is willing to climb himself.

Andrew Carnegie, 1835–1919
Scottish-born American businessman, philanthropist

$\mathcal{I}$ am looking for a lot of men

who have an infinite capacity

to not know what can't be done.

Henry Ford, 1863–1947
American automobile manufacturer

$\mathcal{S}$etting an example

is not the main means

of influencing another;

it is the only means.

Albert Einstein, 1879–1955
German-born American physicist

Example has more followers than reason.

We unconsciously imitate what pleases us

and approximate to the characters we most admire.

Christian Nevell Bovee, 1820–1904
American lawyer, author

A community is like a ship;

everyone ought to be prepared

to take the helm.

Henrik Ibsen, 1828–1906
Norwegian playwright

$\mathcal{W}$hen things go wrong

in your command,

start searching for the reason

in increasingly large circles

around your own desk.

General Bruce Clarke, 1901–1964
American military leader

$\mathscr{T}$he leaders who work most effectively,

it seems to me, never say 'I.' And that's not because

they have trained themselves not to say 'I.'

They don't think 'I.' They think 'we.'

They think 'team.' They understand their job to be

to make the team function.

Peter Drucker, 1909-2005
American management theorist

*I*f people

are coming to work excited … if they're making mistakes

freely and fearlessly … if they're having fun … if they're

concentrating on doing things rather than preparing

reports and going to meetings – then somewhere

you have leaders.

Robert Townsend, b. 1957
American actor

If you set the right example,
you won't need to worry about the rules.

Anonymous

*Leadership should be
more participative
than directive,
more enabling
than performing.*

Mary D. Poole, b. 1938
American writer

Many managers
believe they are communicating with their employees
when in reality they are only talking excessively
and listening for their own words
to be reflected in employees' statements.

Jack Hulbert, 1892–1978
English actor

There is something that is much more scarce,
something far finer, something rarer than ability.

It is the ability to recognize ability.

Elbert Hubbard, 1856–1915
American philosopher, writer

$\mathcal{I}$f it were considered desirable

to destroy a human being,

the only thing necessary would be

to give his work a character of uselessness.

Fyodor Dostoyevsky, 1821–1881
Russian writer

$\mathcal{P}$ull the string,

and it will follow wherever you wish.

Push it,

and it will go nowhere at all.

Dwight D. Eisenhower, 1890–1969
President of the United States of America

$\mathcal{K}$eep your fears to yourself,

but share your inspiration

with others.

Robert Louis Stevenson, 1850–1894
English novelist, poet

It is not fair to ask of others

what you are unwilling to do yourself.

Eleanor Roosevelt, 1884–1962
First Lady of the United States of America, writer, diplomat

$\mathcal{T}$he very essence of leadership

is that you have to have a vision.

Theodore Hesburgh, b. 1917
American clergyman

Opportunity and Risk

In times of change,

learners inherit the earth

while the learned find themselves

beautifully equipped to deal with

a world that no longer exists.

Eric Hoffer, 1902–1983
American writer

'*Impossible*'
is a word found only
in a fool's dictionary.

Napoleon Bonaparte, 1769–1821
French emperor

I am a man

of fixed and unbending principles,

the first of which

is to be flexible at all times.

Everett Dirkson, 1896–1969
United States Senator

*T*he right man

is the one who

seizes the moment.

Johann Wolfgang von Goethe, 1749–1832
German poet, writer, dramatist, scientist

*C*autious, careful people,

always casting about to preserve their reputation

and social standing, never can bring about a reform.

Those who are really in earnest must be willing

to be anything or nothing in the world's estimation

and publicly and privately, in season and out,

avow their sympathy with despised and

persecuted ideas and their advocates

and bear the consequences.

Susan B. Anthony, 1820–1906
American civil rights leader

$\mathcal{D}$on't be afraid

to take a big step if one is indicated.

You can't cross a chasm

in two small jumps.

David Lloyd George, 1863–1945
British Prime Minister

$\mathcal{Y}$ou need the ability to fail.

I'm amazed at the number of organizations

that set up an environment where

they do not permit their people to be wrong.

You cannot innovate unless you are

willing to accept some mistakes.

Charles Knight, 1791–1873
English publisher, writer

The rung of a ladder

was never meant to rest upon

but only to hold a man's foot

long enough to enable him

to put the other

somewhat higher.

Thomas Huxley, 1825–1895
British biologist

$\mathcal{M}$en make history
and not the other way around.
In periods where there is no leadership,
society stands still.
Progress occurs when courageous,
skillful leaders seize the opportunity
to change things for the better.

Harry S. Truman, 1884–1972
President of the United States of America

$\mathcal{G}$od helps those that help themselves.

Benjamin Franklin, 1706–1790
American statesman, scientist

There is a tide in the affairs of men

Which, taken at the flood, leads on to fortune;

Omitted, all the voyage of their life

Is bound in shallows and miseries.

On such a full sea we are now afloat,

And we must take the current when it serves

or lose our ventures.

William Shakespeare, 1564–1616
English poet, playwright

$\mathscr{A}$ wise man

makes more opportunities

than he finds.

Sir Francis Bacon, 1561–1626
English philosopher

*I*f your ship

doesn't come in,

swim out to it.

———

Anonymous

If you wait for
opportunities to occur,
you will be one of the crowd.

Edward de Bono, b. 1933
American psychologist, writer

*T*he best luck of all

is the luck you make for yourself.

General Douglas MacArthur, 1880–1964
American military leader

$\mathcal{T}$o improve the golden moment of opportunity,

and catch the good that is within our reach,

is the great art of life.

William James, 1842–1910
American psychologist, philosopher

I would not creep along that coast but steer

Out in mid-sea by guidance of the stars.

George Eliot, 1819–1880
English novelist, poet

$\mathcal{H}$e that is over-cautious

will accomplish little.

Friedrich von Schiller, 1759–1805
German historian, poet

*T*ake calculated risks.

This is quite different

from being rash.

General George S. Patton, 1885–1945
American military leader

There are risks and costs

to a program of action,

but they are far less than

the long-range risks and costs

of comfortable inaction.

—————————————

John F. Kennedy, 1917–1963
President of the United States of America

$\mathcal{D}$uring the first period of a man's life,

the danger is not to take the risk.

Soren Kierkegaard, 1813–1855
Danish philosopher

There is no security on this earth;

there is only opportunity.

General Douglas MacArthur, 1880–1964
American military leader

*E*ven a mistake may turn out to be

the one thing necessary

to a worthwhile achievement.

_____

Henry Ford, 1863–1947
American automobile manufacturer

How to Get to the Top

*T*here are two kinds of success.

One is the very rare kind that comes to the man who has

the power to do what no one else has the power to do.

That is genius.

But the average man who wins what we call success

is not a genius. He is a man who has merely the

ordinary qualities that he shares with his fellows,

but who has developed those ordinary qualities

to a more than ordinary degree.

Theodore Roosevelt, 1858–1919
President of the United States of America

$\mathcal{D}$o your work

with your whole heart

and you will succeed –

there is so little competition.

Elbert Hubbard, 1865–1915
American writer

*O*ne only gets to the top rung of the ladder

by steadily climbing up, one at a time,

and suddenly all sorts of powers, all sorts of abilities

which you thought never belonged to you,

suddenly become within your own possibility

and you think,

'Well, I'll have a go, too.'

Baroness Margaret Thatcher, b. 1925
British Prime Minister

$\mathcal{W}$atch, listen, and learn.
You can't know it all yourself;
anyone who thinks they do
is destined for mediocrity.

Donald Trump, b. 1946
American real estate magnate

*B*elieve you can, and you can. Belief is one of the most powerful of all problem dissolvers. When you believe that a difficulty can be overcome, you are more than halfway to victory over it already.

———————————————

Norman Vincent Peale, 1898–1993
American writer, minister

I found that the men and women

who got to the top

were those who did the jobs they had in hand

with everything they had of energy

and enthusiasm and hard work.

Harry S. Truman, 1884–1972
President of the United States of America

$\mathcal{T}$he only limit

to our realization of tomorrow

will be our doubts of today.

Let us move forward

with strong and active faith.

Franklin D. Roosevelt, 1882–1945
President of the United States of America

$\mathcal{B}$enefits should be conferred gradually;
and in that way, they will taste better.

Niccolo Machiavelli, 1469–1527
Italian diplomat, political philosopher, writer

Self-trust

is the first secret

of success.

Ralph Waldo Emerson, 1803–1882
American essayist, philosopher

$\mathcal{Y}$ou can close more business deals in two months

by becoming interested in other people

than you can in two years

by trying to get people interested in you.

Dale Carnegie, 1888–1955
American writer

*Always bear in mind
that your own resolution to succeed
is more important than any other.*

Abraham Lincoln, 1809–1865
President of the United States of America

$\mathcal{I}$f you aspire

to the highest place,

it is no disgrace

to stop at the second

or even the third place.

Cicero, 106–43BC
Roman orator, statesman, essayist

I like thinking big.

If you're going to be thinking anything,

you might as well think big.

Donald Trump, b. 1946
American real estate magnate

$\mathscr{E}$ach player must accept

the cards life deals him.

But once they are in hand,

he must decide how to play the cards

to win the game.

Voltaire, 1694–1778
French historian, writer

A creative man is motivated

by the desire to achieve

not by the desire

to beat others.

_____

Ayn Rand, 1905–1982
American writer

*Whether you believe
you can do a thing
or believe you can't,
you are right.*

Henry Ford, 1863–1947
American automobile manufacturer

They are able

who think they are able.

Virgil, 70–19 BC
Roman poet

*N*ever look down to test the ground

before taking your next step;

only he who keeps his eye

fixed on the far horizon

will find his right road.

Dag Hammarskjöld, 1905–1961
Swedish statesman, Secretary-General of the United Nations

*F*ormulate and stamp

indelibly on your mind

a mental picture of yourself

as succeeding.

Hold this picture tenaciously.

Never permit it to fade.

Your mind will seek to develop the picture ....

Do not build obstacles in your imagination.

Norman Vincent Peale, 1898–1993
American clergyman

The victory of success is half won

when one gains the habit

of setting goals and achieving them.

Even the most tedious chore will become endurable

as you parade through each day

convinced that each task,

no matter how menial or boring,

brings you closer to achieving your dreams.

Og Mandino, 1923–1996
American editor, author

*Our aspirations
are our possibilities.*

Samuel Johnson, 1709–1784
English lexicographer, critic, essayist

The heights by men reached and kept

Were not attained by sudden flight,

But they, while their companions slept,

Were toiling upward in the night.

Henry Wadsworth Longfellow, 1807–1882
American poet

*W*hen goals go, meaning goes.

When meaning goes, purpose goes.

When purpose goes,

life goes dead on our hands.

Carl Jung, 1875–1961
Swiss psychiatrist

$\mathcal{T}$o accomplish great things

we must not only act,

but also dream;

not only plan,

but also believe.

Anatole France, 1844–1924
French writer

$\mathcal{D}$o the thing

and you will have

the power.

Ralph Waldo Emerson, 1803–1882
American essayist, philosopher

Flaming enthusiasm,

backed up by horse sense and persistence,

is the quality that most frequently

makes for success.

Dale Carnegie, 1888–1955
American writer

The first requisite for success
is the ability to apply
your physical and mental energies
to one problem incessantly
without growing weary.

Thomas A. Edison, 1847–1931
American inventor

*Y*ou can't build a reputation

on what you're going to do.

Henry Ford, 1863–1947
American automobile manufacturer

$\mathcal{T}$he great end in life

is not knowledge

but action.

Thomas Fuller, 1608–1661
English clergyman, writer

*O*ur great business in life
is not to see what lies dimly at a distance
but to do what lies clearly at hand.

Thomas Carlyle, 1795–1881
Scottish essayist, historian, philosopher

$\mathcal{B}$elieve in the best,

think your best, study your best,

have a goal for your best,

never be satisfied with less than your best,

try your best, and in the long run

things will turn out for the best.

Henry Ford, 1863–1947
American automobile manufacturer

*W*ise Words From Leaders

$\mathcal{T}$he only real security

that a man can have in this world

is a reserve of knowledge,

experience, and ability.

Henry Ford, 1863–1947
American automobile manufacturer

Action

may not always bring happiness,

but there is no happiness

without action.

Benjamin Disraeli, 1808–1881
British Prime Minister

*M*en in general
are quick to believe
that which they desire
to be true.

Julius Caesar, 100–44 BC
Roman emperor

I am an optimist.

It does not seem too much use

being anything else.

Sir Winston Churchill, 1874–1965
British Prime Minister, statesman, writer

$\mathcal{T}$here is one rule for the industrialist and that is:

Make the best quality of goods possible

at the lowest cost,

paying the highest wages possible.

Henry Ford, 1863–1947
American automobile manufacturer

$\mathcal{Y}$ou are remembered
for the rules you break.

General Douglas MacArthur, 1880–1964
American military leader

Your most unhappy customers

are your greatest source of learning.

Bill Gates, b. 1955
American computer software designer, industrialist

*T*ake away my people, but leave my factories,

and soon grass will grow on the factory floors.

Take away my factories, but leave my people,

and soon we will have

a new and better factory.

Andrew Carnegie, 1835–1919
Scottish-born American businessman, philanthropist

Failure is simply

the opportunity to begin again,

this time more intelligently.

———————————

Henry Ford, 1863–1947
American automobile manufacturer

*W*henever you are asked

if you can do a job, tell 'em,

'Certainly I can!'

Then get busy and

find out how to do it.

Theodore Roosevelt, 1858–1919
President of the United States of America

No man is justified in doing evil on the ground of expediency.

Theodore Roosevelt, 1858–1919
President of the United States of America

*We are prone to judge success
by the index of our salaries
or the size of our automobiles
rather than by the quality of our service
and our relationship to humanity.*

Martin Luther King, Jr., 1929–1968
American civil rights leader, minister

$\mathscr{I}$t may be true that the law

cannot make a man love me,

but it can stop him from lynching me,

and I think that's pretty important.

Martin Luther King, Jr., 1929–1968
American civil rights leader, minister

$\mathscr{B}$etter to fight for something
than live for nothing.

General George S. Patton, 1885–1945
American military leader

If freedom of speech is taken away, then,

dumb and silent, we may be led

like sheep to the slaughter.

George Washington, 1732–1799
President of the United States of America

$\mathscr{N}$othing is particularly hard
if you divide it into small jobs.

Henry Ford, 1863–1947
American automobile manufacturer

*N*o man is worth his salt

who is not ready at all times

to risk his body,

to risk his well-being,

to risk his life

to a great cause.

Theodore Roosevelt, 1858–1919
President of the United States of America

My grandfather once told me

that there were two kinds of people:

those who do the work and

those who take the credit.

He told me to try to be in the first group.

There is much less competition.

Indira Gandhi, 1917–1984
Prime Minister of India

$\mathcal{T}$he price of greatness

is responsibility.

Sir Winston Churchill, 1874–1965
British Prime Minister, statesman, writer

*T*ime and money spent

in helping men to do more for themselves

is far better than mere giving.

Henry Ford, 1863–1947
American automobile manufacturer

$\mathcal{I}$s the rich world aware

of how four billion

of the six billion live?

If we were aware,

we would want to help out;

we'd want to get involved.

———————

Bill Gates, b. 1955
American computer software designer, industrialist

The peace we seek,
founded upon decent trust and
cooperation among nations,
can be fortified not by weapons of war
but by wheat and cotton, by milk and wool,
by meat and timber, and by rice.
These are words that translate
into every language.

Dwight D. Eisenhower, 1890–1969
President of the United States of America

*W*hat is the use of living

if not to strive for noble causes

and to make this muddled world a better place

for those who will live in it

after we are gone.

Sir Winston Churchill, 1874–1965
British Prime Minister, statesman, writer

Enough of blood and tears.

Enough.

Yitzhak Rabin, 1922–1995
Israeli Prime Minister

$\mathcal{L}$et there by justice for all.

Let there be peace for all.

Let there be work, bread, water,

and salt for all.

Let each know that for each, the body,

mind, and soul

have been freed to fulfill themselves.

Nelson Mandela, b. 1918
President of South Africa

$\mathscr{P}$eace and justice

are two sides

of the same coin.

Dwight D. Eisenhower, 1890–1969
President of the United States of America

We have the means and capacity

to deal with our problems

if only we can find the will.

Kofi Annan, b. 1938
Ghanian Secretary-General of the United Nations

$\mathcal{L}$et your heart feel

for the afflictions and

distress of everyone,

and let your hand give

in proportion to your purse.

George Washington, 1732–1799
President of the United States of America

*P*eace does not require

that each man love his neighbor –

it requires only that they live together

with mutual tolerance,

submitting their disputes

to a just and peaceful settlement.

John F. Kennedy, 1917–1963
President of the United States of America

I never did anything alone.

Whatever I accomplished

was accomplished collectively.

Golda Meir, 1898–1978
Israeli Prime Minister

I offer neither pay, nor quarters, nor food;

I offer only hunger, thirst, forced marches and death.

Let him who loves his country with his heart,

and not merely with his lips,

follow me.

Garibaldi, 1807–1882
Leader in the unification of Italy

$\mathcal{T}$here is nothing more dangerous

than to build a society

with a large segment of people

who feel they have no stake in it.

People who have a stake in their society

protect that society,

but when they don't have it,

they unconsciously want to destroy it.

Martin Luther King, Jr., 1929–1968
American civil rights leader, minister

*O*bstacles are

those frightful things you see

when you take your eyes

off your goal.

Henry Ford, 1863–1947
American automobile manufacturer

$\mathcal{A}$nd so, my fellow Americans,

ask not what your country can do for you;

ask what you can do for your country.

John F. Kennedy, 1917–1963
President of the United States of America

$\mathscr{T}$he man who has done his level best

is a success,

even though the world may write him down

as a failure.

B.C. Forbes, 1880–1854
Scottish journalist

$\mathscr{I}$ always tell my staff,

'I don't care a damn for your loyalty

when you think I am right.

The time I want it

is when you think I am wrong.'

General Sir John Monash, 1865–1931
Australian military commander

The best way
of avenging thyself
is not to become
like the wrongdoer.

Marcus Aurelius, 121–180
Roman emperor, philosopher

*T*he difference between what we do

and what we are capable of doing

would suffice to solve

most of the world's problems.

_____

Mahatma Gandhi, 1869–1948
Indian political leader

Success

is how hard you bounce

when you hit the bottom.

General George S. Patton, 1885–1945
American military leader

*F*ailure is success

if we learn from it.

———————————

Malcolm Forbes, 1917–1990
American publisher

You know,

by the time you've reached my age,

you've made plenty of mistakes

if you've lived your life properly.

Ronald Reagan, 1911–2004
President of the United States of America

*T*he path we have chosen

for the present is full of hazards

as all paths are.

The cost of freedom is always high,

but Americans have always paid it.

And there is one path we shall never choose,

and that is the path of surrender

or submission.

John F. Kennedy, 1917–1963
President of the United States of America

*F*earlessness may be a gift,

but perhaps more precious

is the courage acquired through endeavor,

courage that comes from cultivating the habit

of refusing to let fear dictate one's actions,

courage that could be described

as 'grace under pressure' – grace which is

renewed repeatedly in the face of harsh,

unremitting pressure.

_____

Aung San Suu Kyi, b. 1945
Burma's democratically elected leader

$\mathcal{N}$othing in the world

can take the place of persistence.

Talent will not; nothing is more common

than unsuccessful men with talent.

Genius will not; unrewarded genius is almost a proverb.

Education will not; the world is full of educated failures.

Persistence and determination alone are omnipotent.

—————————————

Calvin Coolidge, 1872–1933
President of the United States of America

We have to choose between
a global market driven only by
calculations of short-term profit
and one which has a human face.

Kofi Annan, b. 1938
Ghanian Secretary-General of the United Nations

If you want

to make peace with your enemy,

you have to work with your enemy.

Then he becomes your partner.

Nelson Mandela, b. 1918
President of South Africa

I am easily satisfied with the very best.

Sir Winston Churchill, 1874–1965
British Prime Minister, statesman, writer

$\mathcal{I}$ learned that courage

was not the absence of fear,

but the triumph over it.

The brave man is not he

who does not feel afraid, but he

who conquers that fear.

Nelson Mandela, b. 1918
President of South Africa

Never let us negotiate out of fear,

but let us never fear to negotiate.

John F. Kennedy, 1917–1963
President of the United States of America

$\mathcal{T}$he only limit
to our realization of tomorrow

will be our doubts of today.

Let us move forward with

strong and active faith.

Franklin D. Roosevelt, 1882–1945
President of the United States of America